A
MISSPELT
YOUTH

STEPHEN HANSON

PUBLISHED BY
LAPWING PUBLICATIONS
c/o DENNIS & RENE GREIG
1 BALLYSILLAN DRIVE
BELFAST BT14 8HQ

PRINTED BY

TEXTFLOW SERVICES LTD.
MALONE ROAD, BELFAST
TEL; 01232 663591

ISBN 1 898472 22 X

LAPWING POETRY PAMPHLET
Stephen Hanson: A Misspelt Youth
PUBLISHED 1995

Lapwing Publications gratefully acknowledge the financial assistance of the Arts Council of Northern Ireland and The UK Foundation for Sport and the Arts in the publication of this pamphlet.

CONTENTS

for DAVID

HARD WORDS

Ten words a day, from
'The Oxford School Spelling Book'.
Evenings learning
Dividing into smaller words,
Writing them in yellow chalk,
On an old grey blackboard
'Til I had them off by rote

By morning they'd smeared away.
A damp cloth of chalky dust.
Chew them again with cornflakes,
To melt in the grit of sugar-milk.

Three out of ten on Monday,
Four on Tuesday.
By the end of the week,
Fifteen correct from fifty,
So to the Headmaster for motivation.

Standing in line with the slow and idle,
Just boys.
"You're lazy Hanson,
You'll never make anything of yourself
Hold it higher....
Now the other.....
Do better."

Back to work, at that slim,
Red and black, bruise coloured book.
So many words that all say stupid,
And taste like blood in your mouth.

Twenty years later,
He's still the Head,
A silent advocate for corporal punishment,
"It never did any harm".

DO NOT PASS GO
(for David who died November 1985)

You always took the racing car,
Never robbed the bank,
And only argued once, over Park Lane.

"Think big, go for the best",
But I preferred the terrier,
Liked the sound of Old Kent Road,
The Angel Islington.

No aspirations past owning four stations
And maybe a utility or two.

IT IS YOUR BIRTHDAY David,

I would that you could collect £10,
But you've lost this time.

I sold your car, burnt the board,
Scattered Chance in the park...
You paid too much.

HERE BE DRAGONS

In dragon flight
With Lockheed thrust
Boeing 737 (400)
Fly be wire
Trial by fire
Five hours Belfast
To burning beach

280 deep breathe take-off
Hold invisible hands
Dream of lotions
Hope Dragon knows
What it's doing

WINGS OF DAEDALUS

Fields red, more than mountain's height below.
Milky moon, cataract in midday blue sky.
Us, the silver dot, chased by sun,
Leaving a tear track behind.
Look down, geography lesson landscape,
Coloured, in Caran D'Ache, delicate, neat.

The wind, five hundred knots across wings
That quiver pleasure, at each change of pressure.
A sea below, all laughter line waves, says
Fly high Icarus, enjoy the sun.
Down there, a bleached bird-shit island,
Too far south for proper trees.
A change of note, a change of tilt.
The feathers droop and in we come.

A GIRL CALLED SPRING

Sitting, with you talking,
I can see the sun in your eyes
Before you blink.
Yet you hide it, behind the moon
Of a long winter eclipse.

In the garden,
Beneath packed frost,
There is movement.
Growth smelling of newness,
The ice turns.

Your sun comes out
For these little ones,
Warming them to strength.
In this work, you rise brighter,
Each day higher, each day longer.

Here outside your garden
The light shines too,
Softening colours from greys to yellow.
You are the girl with spring in you.

EQUINOX

Two minutes
That's how much daylight
We lost today
To make this the equinox
Then the balance shifts
Down we go into winter

Today on that last brighter day
I sit at the picture window
Parody of a Dutch whore
Red light over the church
Draws indiscreet shadows on
My neck and face

Climbing the drive
A black crucifix
Flicks across your cheek
But you don't see it and smile
Moving out of the firing line
The sun drops into cover
As I answer the door

Dark now, storm coming
First clouds wet the tea of it
A strong cup, sour aroma
Bitter rain to follow

Now you must decide
You waver, uncertain equinox
Seconds, minutes
Two of them
The balance shifts
You take off your coat
Sun crossed the equator
We turn off the lights

SOLSTICE

While fat little bums of rain
Jiggled along the window frame
Three musicians sat in my summer house

The first played guitar
Notes faster than the shower
Delicate as the touch of grass

Another breathed to a tin whistle
In rhythms of water down glass
Softly lifting drops back to the clouds

The last paddled the bodhran
A hundred children jumping puddles
Would sound the same

We danced barefoot on the lawn
Green to the ankles wet cotton between us
Water pearls in your hair

That night angels jostled on the slates
When we made love
In through the open light they came
Touched your back with their wings
While at a distance three musicians
Played another air

SUMMER COLOURS

The sun rose Pyrite in a Lapis sky
Filled with cotton jet trails
I look up wonder at the net they weave
You stir in your sleep
Put a hand on my chest Move your head
Hair tickling my chin
Brings me back to better things

Morning's almost gone now
The shadow's short and hard
Remind me of men who beat drums
For two months Bandsmen rule the road
And I can't tell the colours from each other

Last night I watched you paint again
A lily and shamrock intertwined
Both white
A single drop of rain on each
The moon turned all to monochrome
You straddled me just shades and light
Moving slowly softly phosphorescent

The sun is past its prime
And we lie here catching rays
Somewhere someone plays a flute
The piper's back in town.

WINTER PATH

Across the frozen stream
Stands a tree, an old tree,
From before the forest fell.
Alone among drystone walls
And limestone scattered fields.

I think of my hand in your glove.
A winter day on this path,
With the sky broken to snow,
Its flakes in your hair.

Down at the lake we watched
Them fall, like spring flies
For deep sleeping trout below.
No swans upon the pitted surface.
Reed beds motionless and waiting.

Silence held misty breath
Between our lips, before they met,
Embraced.
You saw a monk on the crannog.
Watching,
You could always see further than me.

I look again at the tree,
Feel for its loss.
I turn from cold towards the house
And the fire you've lit inside.

EBB TIDE

Sit on the rocks, let time's engine slow,
Let your heart beat with the waves,
Move as they ebb years back.
To this place before we were young.

Spray buttressed cliffs, little changed,
But over the headland invaders see no light.
We are not here, only our spirits
Watch father's six times father come ashore.

Yearly he broke this land and it broke him,
Laid down by a weight of twenty acres toil.
His son buried him on top of Thompson's hill.
The cross they carved from Scottish stone.

As pebbles tide rattle down the shore,
We move quick through years of
Work and pain, pain and death, death and birth,
And all through it all there is this land.

Twenty acres, cliff to track, between streams.
Thin soil over basalt, poor for all but sheep.
Still we watch men go to fight for it.
Dirt from local boots in foreign battle fields.

See father build our new home beside the old
And Tommy from Portmuck painting it yellow.
Remember this from childhood and watch again.
It hurts more to look now that they've gone.

The turning tide has beaten us back to here
And in the real world take a walk with me
Along these cliff top paths, hold my hand.
We'll watch the ferries sail into the mist.

In the dark, before the new moon has risen
You see the sweep of lights from the road.
Reflect on the sold sign by the gate.
Our spirits guard tomorrow's tide alone.

CROSSING ONE

Scream in the still air of a sound proof room,
No one hears.
The walls are thick with padded layers of guilt and fear,
No one hears.
Your gagged and choked on wedding vows you now regret,

From the corner of the room walks a red spider,
A pin-head dot crossing the floor.
You stop, just to catch your breath
And the spider says,
"I hear you."

CROSSING BETWEEN 1 AND 2

It's funny how I love you yet we don't touch,
Weeks and weeks go by, we still hold back.
I long to hold you, close the distance,
But still you close your eyes and step away,
The skies cloud over and hide the light of you.

I want to tell you that I love you, will you listen?
This isn't a love song it's a poem, it means more,
The freedom of words to tell what I never say.

Dream I was in the place, before you wake
An angel without wings, I want to fly for you
Brush your skin with pinions of joy, feathers
White and smooth, answers I don't have.

Will you listen I'll explain, in words I don't understand?
With love you can never hold, for holding burns the sky
How can an angel fly, burn, love and die
Yet through it all, all in all, I love you and I'll fly.

CROSSING TWO

Come with me,
Leave your husband behind,
We'll take to the west
Go back to my home.

Cross the border,
That puts you with him
Makes me a foreigner,
Then we can make this journey.

By eleven the city's behind us,
Overnight rain clearing,
But cumulus of doubt
Still shades your eyes.

Your wedding ring, is
Chained gold at your neck,
How heavy does it lie?
Only the lighter shadow,
Shows it gone from your hand.

At lunch in Swanlinbar, you sit
With your back to the phone,
Looking at it in the mirror
Behind my head.
Dialling numbers in the salad
With your fork.

Over the Shannon at Carrick,
The road draws on,
Spins the world
Under our wheels,
Pulling the day this way.

In evening's water-colour light
We cross the island bridge,
Pass a storm-worn man,
Pushing a black bicycle.
Mizzling salt,
Blurs his existence.
Leaving us alone to the road,
That narrows, climbs and dips.
Over the headland
To the last bay at Keem.

The beach is Autumn empty,
No one to heed the shingle's
Brittle innuendoes
As we search out driftwood.
The wind pinches colour
To your cheeks,
Pushed us closer,
Flinging strands of your hair
In my mouth.

We climb to the ridge,
West, the low sun
Slows above the ocean.

I turn from the light,
Blink you into focus
And watch the reflection fade.
Today from this hilltop,
You were the last person
In Europe to see the sun.
Part of it will stay with you.

CROSSING THREE

Your rosary glints,
In the cold electric
Light of Jesus.

I, wrapped in agnostic quilt
Dream of last night's pieta

SPRING CLEAN

I'd take up this Wilton World, hang it,
Beat it 'til the war dust had blown away
Tack it back to Europe's floor
Smoothing history's rucks of hatred
Once a week I'd shake 'n' vac
To keep stubborn smells at bay.

CONS AND PROS

I live in a third floor room near Kings Cross
The only luxury a four foot cast iron balcony
On summer nights when breezes blow hot
From the roofs of air conditioned buildings
I sit out there head against the bars and listen to the
G.P.O. vans driving through cooling tar to the sorting office
Below night traders do deals in cars from Mercs to Minis
The cons and pros and junkies are window shopped by
crawlers

Across the street is Bridie from Athlone
Playing tricks in a basement stair-well
She lives in the attic above me but works
On the street to keep the landlady happy

She sees me watching and grins
While squeezing the last pennies worth
Before tying the knot
The Jon thinks the smile's for him and tips well
She waves the note at me as he pulls up his zip
Lifts up his Standard and walks stone necked away

It's strange how far down someone seems from the third
floor
Though I'm not so high myself as I contemplate
Prose and poetry within the glimpse of Kings Cross
Where later a girl is stabbed the third this week

Today Bridie up and left for home
Saying "If you're ever in Athlone..."
And away to the river and the rain
And the Barrowlands
Raising her standards with her rucksack

The air is thicker tonight harder on the lungs
Thunder in the distance taunts and disappoints
While the red vans rumble round
In and out of my head

I lift from my body drift out the window and up
Up on the hot winds blowing from the city towers
Up until the black sky below thins
And the street lights above constellations
That flicker in a haze
The city is ten million suns and there's no sign

CRUISING

Friday's dawn mist clears above the jetty,
Its last remnants edge into my head,
Mixing half-memories with déjà vu.

The boat in other times, with other people,
Gone now by choice or accident.
Map of nostalgia unfolding along worn creases,
Navigation through life.

Cruising brings me back, unwinds the spring
That pushes always to the future.
Back into a past of verdant islands,
Splashes of delight to rediscover.

At night, in downy arms of quilt,
I listen to the lovers, wind and Lough,
Feel the tremor of their rhythm
Through the hull.

With tight shut eyes, I weave your picture
In old light, behind my lids.
In the morning autumn rain flows by,
Today I go the other way.

YACHTS

He sits on the wall where the sea's
Now a car park, looking out,
As if the Fords were yachts.
Bottle braced between knees
Of well worn brown corduroy.
Black shoe heels scuffing tunes
On stones, where boys with
Rods passed summer days.

He watches her tack round bumpers,
Buffeted by winds, only in her head.
Cheeks puffed red against the cold,
Or with today's Brew.
Gloves, over hands like gloves,
Clutching precious cargo, a child
Perhaps? Pale skinned.

A leaf drifts by, green edged
Memory of days long passed,
Drinking for pleasure,
With steady hand and clear eye.
Sad smile at a hand, fingers
Round the long smooth neck.
Swift chug. Almost choking.
Leaf drifts on and thought with it.

THE SALAD

Take a two masted yawl,
Sail south on the rim of Europe.
In Morocco gather bulgar wheat,
Lift the chaff to desert winds,
Blow.

Over the Aegean to Greece
Climb a hot limestone escarpment
Pick black olives, smell the sunlight
Taste the dried mountain air,
Follow me.

Sail to southern Spain,
Through strong salt seas.
Take tomatoes fresh, red,
Colour of Spanish soil.
Sail on.

At the mouth of the Seine,
Stop at Honfleur,
Above the quay, at the shop,
Buy fresh vinaigrette.
Catch the tide.

We sail west, over the edge.
In the galley, soak bulgar wheat,
Sieve through Damask muslin.
As the boat shifts and dips,
Mix all together.

Under the stern lantern,
Dusk catches us,
We eat together,
From the same bowl.

THE PROBLEM IS ALL INSIDE YOUR HEAD

Scratching guitar strings, the tramp looked into me.
His hair, long beaded tangled abacus,
Account of last month on the street,
Each colour a number, a note in the song,
Fifty ways to leave your lover.

Nearly three weeks he's sung this song
Each day as I pass,
On long walk through piss stained subway
Of blue tiles and limescale mushrooms,
Where queues of old graffiti mumble threats.

Behind sound of rats, scuttling between frets,
Chords without melody wavering into semi-tones,
Bronchial lungs lift acid words to my guilty back,
Fifty ways to leave your lover.

NIGHT CHILLS

Tomorrow, early, you'll take the Dart
up from the Southside,
cross the Liffey by Custom House Quay,
into Connolly Station.
As the sun lifts above the stockyard,
catching the whiteness of frosted breath,
you'll wait for the Northbound train.

Remember us at the barrier
I leaving for Belfast, you staying for work.
"Think I'm catching a cold" you said.
I know the symptoms.

It's three-fifteen and black as Dalkey Island.
Through the chills of a rising temperature,
I turn on the light, lift down the map
and spread it on the floor.
Dun Laoghaire's below my breast bone.
In Mount Merrion, this side of my shoulder,
between Greenfield and Trees Road,
I'll find you.
There, in that pink square near church and park.
Can you hear my heart beat,
only three inches to the mile away.

This past week I haven't forgotten your crew cut hair,
has it grown? Are your cheeks flushed,
have you sniffed and sneezed?
Are you awake now with night chills,
looking at a map of Belfast,
as the sweat dries on you.

Tomorrow we will wrap together in fifteen togs of heat.
Drink honey and lemon from big stone mugs
and feel much better.

OMEGA'S BIRTH

In the first storm of the new Ice Age,
They lay together, woman and man.
While sleet ripped the soil,
Her body rhythm moved to perfection.
Trees fell, powerlines failed,
Two pronuclei fused into a nucleus.

At Hinkley Point U238 escapes into the sea.
Day 14 the heart is formed, but does it beat?
Chloroflurocarbon drifts skyward, choking air
One month, now we see your hands and feet.
Burning trees hide the sun, burn some more.
Two months tells us your a girl.

The earth turns round the sun and you
Turn too, dancing at night while she sleeps.
Sweet rain falls bitter on the land,
While you grow on, in waters of life.

Full term, breeched and hard,
Her pain is long, but you are born.
With eyes unfocused see what we have done.
Surely you have come too late,
Even so, come.

MAN OF THE HILLS

My father dies tomorrow, or the next day.
With family here around him, yet alone.
His glazed eyes see much further than this room.

Perhaps he stands upon the tor at Bernagh,
Gazing down to the Blue Lough's sheen.
Where peat hags ruck the landscape,
Broken only by the river and the track.
On cloudless days we walked the paths to heaven,
It seems much closer now.

The man who climbed the hills,
Lies frail between the sheets
That will soon be a shroud.